A Question of Time

A Question of Time

Poems by

Kathleen A Dale

Cover design by Shay Culligan
Author photo by Kathleen A Dale
Cover image by Kay Sage

ISBN: 978-1-63980-536-5

Kelsay Books
502 South 1040 East, A-119
American Fork, Utah 84003
Kelsaybooks.com

for Steve

Acknowledgments

The following poems first appeared, sometimes in slightly different form or with a different title, in the following journals and anthologies:

Centrifugal Eye: "Sonata," "Evergreen," "She Folds Laundry"
Chiron Review: "without desire," "Mixing Cement"
Free Verse: "The Apparent Immortality of Things"
Gathering Place of the Waters—Anthology of Milwaukee Poets 2017: "Scheherazade"
Great Lakes Review: "Quivira"
The Lyric: "there is a wilderness"
The Orchards Poetry Journal: "First Dive" ("At Seventy"), "A Question of Art," "She Watches Her Hands," "Hunger & Mercy," "directions for playing"
Plainsong: "Telling the Truth"
Poems for Malala anthology: "Wild Rhubarb"
Poetry and Physics: "She Ponders Questions of Quantum Physics"
Rattle: "Tying the Knot," "A Question of Time"
Syncopation Literary Journal: "'Round Midnight," "Delicate Instruments," "For Pianist Mitsuko Uchida"
Verse Wisconsin: "Rose Sacrament"
Wisconsin People and Ideas: "The Self-Organizing Universal Nail Salon," "Palimpsest: Painting Her Again," "Homeless in August"

Other poems in this edition first appeared in the author's previous books and chapbooks:

"Family Snapshot," "After Easter Sunday, 1956," "Leavening," "She Folds Laundry," "Forty Years of Love," "The Craft," "Escape: Spring, 1926," "Evergreen," "Gate Screener," "Rescue," "Picking Peaches"

Cover Image Permission

Permission to use Kay Sage's "The Great Impossible" 1961 (medium: watercolor and charcoal on cut-and-pasted paper with glass lenses and cut-and-pasted printed paper on paper) is granted by

and by

Kay Sage was an American Surrealist artist and poet active between 1936 and 1963. For more information about her life and work, please see:

www.thecollector.com/kay-sage-paintings-artists-and-death/

Other Books by the Author

Chapbooks of Poetry

Tying the Knot
Rescue Mission
Avatars of Baubo

Other Books

The Beautiful Unnamed (poetry)
Offerings: The Decluttering of a Life (autobiography)

Contents

Part Three: A Question of Time

Foreword

The phrase "A Question of Time" has accrued many meanings for me. As I've compiled this collection of poems ranging from 1969 to the present, it of course refers to the changes that both I and my poetry have undergone—not only the time needed for personal growth and that which comes from practicing an art but also the additions to my poetic style—reflecting, partly, what I was reading at the time. First, there were the mainly male, modern American poets that I studied for my PhD—imagistic, lyrical, metaphoric, not clearly personal; then the rise of Adrienne Rich, Sylvia Plath, and Anne Sexton in the 70s and their much-maligned 'confessional' poems which, in fact, led to today's popular personal narrative poetry. At that time I became a founding member of the Milwaukee chapter of the Feminist Writers' Guild—a writing group which met for many years.

I have been wanting to publish a second full-length book of poetry. The more I thought about it, the unpublished poems I wrote from 1969 through 2000 came to mind. During that time, I was pursuing academic graduate work and then teaching English Composition and Literature—for a short time in high school but for a much longer time on the freshman college level. Until I retired in 2006 my poetry was composed mostly on office computers after I had finished teaching, meeting students, and grading papers for the day.

I found that my topics have not changed very much over the six decades I have been writing poetry (my first poem, "Summer," was published when I was eleven in the Girl Scout magazine *The American Girl*). As a teen, I started writing to come to terms with my sister's death from polio in 1952 when she was sixteen and I was seven. Later, in my 30s and 40s, writing poem after poem about her death was a kind of therapy which replaced the space left by a literal Christianity with a more transcendent view. Once I resumed piano lessons in 2007 and joined another poets' group about the same time, both my playing and my writing began to take more public forms.

The disciplines of both poetry and the piano (which I began studying at seven) led me through to a more complex view of many topics. I wrote about music and art; I wrote about the earth and the smaller world around me; I wrote about time.

As I started to think more about this new book, I placed the old and the newer poems next to each other as I sorted them into the themes listed above, regardless of dates. Here, I have included the original dates of the poems as well as any revision dates. I find it interesting to see how much both my style and my perspectives have evolved. About half of the poems here have been published—either in literary journals, anthologies, and/or in my three chapbooks and one full-length book of poetry.

I want to thank Ruth Pszwaro, artistic director of the Grand Marais Art Colony in Minnesota, for offering me the Belvo-Jorgenson Residency Scholarship so that I could spend a week in that beautiful, quiet space—writing, revising, sorting through, and organizing poetry from the past 50+ years.

What has emerged for me is a kind of story, moving from the 'world'—its joys and sorrows, to 'art'—its ability to transform and heal, to 'time'—its mystery and how it may be something entirely different from what we have come to believe.

Nothing is ever over, nothing is ever ended,
and worlds open up within the world we know.
—Lee Smith, *Oral History*

Un poème n'est jamais terminé, juste abandonné.
—Paul Valéry

A poem is never finished. . . .

Part One: The Question of the World

Escape: Spring, 1926

Blood begins to soar
at sight of the windsock
forever filled with possibility.

Of those kindled by Kitty Hawk,
whose imaginations feathered and flamed,
my father, 17, assembles oilcloth,
balsa wood, wire in the tractor shed.

For days he leaves only to eat and sleep,
dreaming of clouds and listening
to the incessant south wind.

He saves for a polished propellor,
mounts and oils it, spins it down
into a roaring disk, importantly slips
glass goggles over his eyes.

Slowly the fragile contraption
bumps to life, shudders
along prairie grass,
raises its tail and flies!

Round faces turn up like flowers to the
dipping wings buzzing the frame farmhouse.

Catching a thermal, he floats
for the first time ever over oceans of fields
rolling with heavy wheat.

Seeing them from the air loosens his soul,
changes his bearings. Never again
will he be bound to his father's land
in the same way.

1998–2023

First Dive

At seventy, the thing she wanted
to learn was to dive:

to tuck her chin to her chest, between
her outstretched arms and to fall

headfirst toward the bottom she had both
feared and yearned for since she had

first seen water—the still pool
untouched, unrippled, heavy with meaning

and promise: to feel its cool caress, hear
the bubbles of breath leave her body, see

the illusion of being enclosed utterly by blue;
to know that she could aim her body down,

then up, and it would joyously comply,
her remaining breath buoying her up, up,

up to break the surface of the old familiar
world as if rising from sleep; it was something

like flying, she thought, something like
taking off from one medium and trying on

another, shedding one set of rules for a second:
one which both frightened and enthralled,

a kind of life to which she had always been born,
on the edge of which she has been forever poised.

2015–2023

22

Red Squirrel at Spring Equinox

It is non-negotiable, loss.
It is the memory of last spring.
It is the not-remembering of many others.

This cold March wind is merciless,
both inflicting pain and moaning,
its crying ceaseless, an anxious child
who will not be comforted, whose parents
will eventually shut her out, as have I,
here at the breakfast table,
drinking my morning coffee.
                                        Outside,
banks of stiff snow slowly drain
to starched lace, emptying like
the bones of old women.

Today's slight red squirrel, first this winter, prances
with all the entitlement of youth to the melted
bowl of water on my deck to drink her fill.

The heavy grey squirrels wrap like slugs
round the cylinder of seed, suck at its teats.

I'm not sure, but it might have been last spring
when I first saw the flock of robins fly fully formed
from the upturned hat of the apparently empty elm.

For sure, the redwings usually trill by my birthday.
But these days it seems nothing's for sure.

The smallest grey has lost part of her tail,
shrinks back as the largest males devour the nut-buttered
bread, barking at her if she ventures close.

Yes, *non-negotiable* might as well be stamped
on all our bills of loss, though none of that matters
in the largest image we have, delivered, today,
on the flimsy, front page of the *Times:*

the infra-red egg of the cosmos, 13.8 billion years old.
From that vantage, filling my second cup,
drinking it in, it is easy to discern balance,
flow, even if it is forever slow in coming.

One grieves. One forgets.
The past streams out behind us, 68 percent dark matter.

But today the sun shines
on a slender red squirrel, drinking crusts
of melted ice, perhaps
mother of the three that walked right
up to our toes last summer and which we,
being ignorant but wanting to help,
drove to the Shelter.

The wild gust of *now* doesn't seem to care
about its eventual passing.

It seems to know how to fall, how
to fail, how to play by the deepest,
the most intricate, the most
arcane rules of the game.

2013–2023

there is a wilderness

there is a wilderness at edge of house
in small unmanaged shadows of neglect
where paint begins unseen to loosen or
a few weeds grow or unpruned boughs dip low
it can be glimpsed through unwashed windows where
things show not totally themselves and at
the backs of fallow cupboards or in shade
beneath trees left to sprout at will
through holes in fallen fences or around
the rumpled rooms of those allowed to dally

only when flown there by the untamed wind
it trusts will it readily root in pots
or blow the breath of time into the sweet
uncultivated cup of your hand

2005

Hunger & Mercy

We must have mercy on the crow that invades a nest of sparrows,
nips off a head, then flies back for more.
The crow is hungry. It is natural.

Deliver us from our enemies.

We must remember to have mercy on the hawk who gladly
gulps down a whole nest of crows.
The hawk is hungry. She was made that way.

Give us this day our daily bread.

But what of those with a mere appetite for veal—
culled from its mother, slaughtered, renamed?

This is my body; remember me.
What of those who snatch hungry nurslings from breasts
at our borders? Have they no mercy?

They know not what they do.
All shot through with the same stardust, we seem to be terrifying
mysteries: black holes of craving and fear.
Forgive us our trespasses.

And the virus without a mouth that stops the breath of a child?
Is it, too, hungry? It knows nothing. Nothing of mercy.

May we make art out of sorrow.

A grey, black, and rust milk snake slips silent into a house
of wrens.

The surviving parents flee to a high branch, keening,
though to us it sounds just like song.

2022

Warning: Graphic Content

The mice came in hordes that fall—
maybe it was the bird seed outside
the kitchen window or the sacks
of snacks we left uncovered.

They ate apples, chewed through
bread wrappers, leaving
a trail of urine for others to follow
through the walls, down to the laundry,
up along the chimney to a bedroom.

I find ads for poison that leads
to internal bleeding after a few days.
But if that mouse is then eaten by a hawk,
the bird dies too.

The pest control man suggests spin traps
—one per mouse—that smash its head in,
but you never have to see it.

Sticky glue boards are as they sound—
mice struggle until they die.

I choose the old-fashioned snap trap,
check them daily, wear gloves to open the wire
that had quickly, cleanly broken the small spine.

Except for the one I set in a bedroom.
Next day it's gone. No trap. No mouse.

No problem.

Except that, when I get down on hands and knees
and look under the bed, there, the rest of the trap still
clamps one foot of the creature that had crawled there,
away from the pain, taken god knows
how long to die.

2023

27

Hearing Aids

Now I can hear

each separate leaf
move against another on the summer
maple this June afternoon.

A screen door slams several houses away.

There are the high voices of children.

Someone has tuned the radio to a Brewers game.

A bird lands on the edge of the birdbath and takes
two or three drinks before she notices me and the dog.
In a two-second whir of wings she is two
streets over.

Last night I lay awake rehearsing a hard thing
I thought I would have to say the next morning.

Turns out, I could just listen.

2023

Evergreen

i.
From branch to stem to needle we grow,
shoots predictable and unpredictable as stars.

Her winter garden hisses with snow
rattling bleached bones of cone-

flower and verbena, cowled
roses dark in their March hollows,

goldenrod roots tangled,
massed under the frozen crust.

Second full moon in March,
blue moon suddenly blooms

like the first moon flower
on a trellis, climbing an

invisible vine. Such moons
she has always watched swell and

wane, hoping that in their dark
doubled ridges, the things she planted

would thrive. But Athena still springs
full blown from her father's bright

brow, no mother to let her
lag, wax slowly, muse,

be a little girl whose dreams
grow new rooms looming

suddenly past the wall where before
there was no door

but now are rooms within rooms,
fractal rooms of infinite length.

We have not dreamed large enough.

ii.
Twilight dallies with the toes of girls
loafing on curbs, brown arches caressing
dust.

Small green doublets of sunflowers,
sprung volunteer, turn likewise,
young,

blind, to setting sun. Full
moon rises unseen
over the stems of

their backs, in the east, dawning.
Inside, she washes dishes at
her kitchen sink.

Her heart rises, glimpsing moon's porcelain
globe before it cracks among trees.
She turns

back to rinse the precision of
each white cup, hangs the blue
linen cloth

carefully to dry, slips out
to calmed dusk to idle with her daughters
dreaming a garden.

iii.
She muses: we thought
the world would change,
we young and noisy feminists,

but we have slackened,
the waves subdued now,
an occasional stridency

swallowed, like a gull's
cry by the dark.
But today somewhere

a woman's clitoris was sliced
from her body, some-
where tonight a woman

walking stares at
a radium-infested field,
somewhere today

a caged dog was killed
by white coats,
somewhere tonight

are women and their daughters
draped and locked away
from sight of men and moon.

iv.
Receding snow releases scent of broken
spruce boughs brooding over red

fists and then the softening mudras of peony
stems as well as small carcasses gathered

lovingly to earth. The living dog
lying in spring sun licks the crevices and

furrows of her palm and so weaves
kith into the woof of poem just as

earth weaves death into the warp of
spring. The girls go on playing

with dust and the woman with water and
from their play rises creation that matters

the world, which withers without the muddy
juice of their play though it lead to nothing

but deep winding pleasure. Earth opens
to the dark newness of moon and to green

seeds ever so small they vanish,
shoots of stars, into the vast imaginary

lines of her palm. She folds leeway
back into her veins, does not term

her creations but dreams lavish
iterated wonder into moon's

blue light, which, rising
ever again and new, wicks the world.

ca. 1995–2000

32

Fantasy at Mt. Rushmore

I cleave to the side of the mountain
on which no women's faces are carved,
veins of rock rigid against my cheek.
As if blind, I translate by touch,
sculpting with my body,
sensing rather than seeing spirits
within rifts of stone.

I move from toehold to fingerhold,
with no harness or sling, only the heat
of balance between me and the terror
of falling, only balance
to reveal the women within the rock—
not carved, blasted, imposed—
but there to my fingertips,
comforting and fluid as clouds.

An ancient Venus, faceless,
rests me on her breasts and belly
like a child just born;
willowy Kuan Yin arches against me,
pointing to heaven, then down to loops—
handholds in her garment for me to grasp;
the face of my friend, older now,
musing, waiting to cross a street,
unaware I am near;
the face of my dead sister, forgotten,
momentarily rises before sinking
again into stone; my mother's face
alight and at peace at long last with forgiveness;
the face of a woman I might have loved,
thrown back in ecstasy.

1993–2023

33

A Hundred Years

My ten-year-old father poses with his baseball team,
nine Kansas farm boys in overalls and mean expressions,
strong-armed, caps on backwards. The wheat field stretches out far
behind them to the next windbreak of cottonwoods; that morning
they had milked, mucked, hayed, or helped to bale.

My father feared horses—maybe he was kicked or bitten,
I never asked and he never said—which was why he never
took to farming. In 1919 there were no tractors, no
combine harvesters. Horses did everything.

Baseball was supposed to be fun but also to teach boys
how to keep going even when losing, not to give up,
not to show feelings; to back up the other guy, to practice
that swing or that throw, over and over, to learn
patience, to inspire respect if not fear.

I never asked my father and he never said
if, the year he was nine, he'd heard of Shoeless Joe Jackson:
the "Black Sox" throwing the World Series.
Would he have been surprised? Would he have cared?
Or having himself played, would he have already learned
about those forces always straining, needing to be checked?

As a young man he tinkered with different forces for fun—
a single-engine plane he learned to fly at the one-windsock-airport,
learning to respect the wind, how to use it to recover from spins
      and stalls,
how to jolt his parents by flying low and barnstorming the farm,
then pulling up and away, waggling his wings.

He eloped with my mother at 21 and climbed telephone poles
for a living until the cigarettes he started smoking at twelve
cut down his air. By 35 he was no longer able to climb or run.
Became a supervisor.

Baseball became a thing of the past, to listen to on the radios
he made at home: crystal sets, then ones with vacuum tubes,
then on the simple TV he devised for everyone in town
to gather around and watch.

He didn't live to see Walter Cronkite break the news
of baseball's later scandals: Pete Rose's betting in '89,
the managers' collusion and players' strike in '94,
cocaine, amphetamines ("greenies"), steroids, or,
after the millennium, Human Growth Hormone
providing that extra edge.

I don't know what he'd think of that or
of giving growth hormones to cows whose milk
would be passed along to children.

Baseball taught boys to compete, to win, to keep
what was their own. Yet my father left the legacy
of the farm to his brother, preferring controllable,
fixable motors to unpredictable horses:
engines in Model Ts and monoplanes,
electricity and all the devices through which one
could skillfully harness its fearsome power.

He never said if he missed baseball, but tonight,
his great-grandson, one hundred years his junior,
in grass-stained uniform and cleats, poses
for my smartphone with his teammates
before the game.

Nine years old, he hits a double—
batting two runs in—then scores on another play;
bats left-handed (never chases balls in the dirt),
steals like a showman. Chews Double Bubble
just like his heroes who make all that money,
all those million-dollar salaries.

He's learning to compete like a man.
We stand up, cheer him on.
"Farm team" means something different now.
(Scouts may be among the fans, watching.)

There haven't been work horses on farms
for a hundred years. Despite air-conditioned
tractor cabs, farmers need second jobs, can't compete
with the corporations buying up family farms.
A single man can't make a living raising wheat,
not even with pesticides, can't keep going even when losing,
can't keep what's his own, dare not show his fear and rage
except maybe to God after a hailstorm flattens his wheat.

I can maybe guess what my father thought of that,
though he never said. I never asked.

My father only had daughters, granddaughters.
He never said and I never asked if he wanted sons.
But on this beautiful June evening I feel
his rare mix of pleasure and envy beside me
on the plank bleacher as his great-grandson—
who makes things too, does math in his head,
beats me at chess, is scrupulously honest—
fields the ball then throws to first,
ending the game.

I'm pretty sure I know what my father would think
of *this* boy—whose middle name is the same as his last—
running up to us sweaty and tired, grinning,
cap on backwards, still relishing all the rewards
of America's greatest game.

2019

Gate Screener

"Fuckin' Arabs!" the old man spits
at me as he dumps his cell phone, keys,
money clip, belt buckle and tin of Skoal
into the bin before he swaggers
through the metal detector ninety minutes

before the start of the Brewers game.
It is late in the season with little chance
at the playoffs. But he's here early
no doubt remembering the days when,
despite fascists and communists, he could

simply stroll into County Stadium, pick
a bleacher, light a Camel, pop a Bud, and
enjoy the game on a Saturday afternoon
with other guys just like himself.
"People!" my partner Manuel and I laugh

before the next group, drunken tailgaters,
sway at our flow-stopping dam before
staggering toward the beautiful green diamond.
Before the next wave of fans, Manny—
usually a joker—tells me quietly

of the hot air balloon trip
he and his wife, who has MS, took
down the length of the Nile last June.
It was amazing to see, he said, the lush
green rising from each bank

but then behind it sand, sand, only
sand as far as they could see. The fertile
delta had shrunk, the cleansing floods
harnessed by the great dam downriver.
"This would never stop a terrorist," an off-

duty cop interrupts, sweeping
his hand around, plopping his badge and wallet
into my cracked plastic bin before
sauntering through. "Thank you for keeping us safe,"
smiles a young father. I smile back,

and let his family's small contraband
of Pepsi can, tiny pocket knife
and pepper spray forgotten on the keychain
of the elegant pregnant woman wearing
a sand-colored hijab sail right through.

2019

Common Midwestern Spiders

We have the bodies we have.

Mine is seven decades old with heavy,
no-longer-suckled breasts and the belly of my mother
though it folds over three Caesarean scars.

The rest of me is scrawny and mostly wrinkled.
My skin is thin. Bruises bloom at the slightest
bump. I wish my boundaries would become tough
as elephant hide or the bark of an oak.

The markings on the large black spider crawling
on the ceiling where I was a guest last night may
have been a Black Widow, according to the internet,
but resembled more the pale hat of the Eastern
Parson, not the red hourglass of Time.

I feared her only because she was too fast
to catch and release. When she fell, she
scurried under the dresser.

By now wide awake, I read that
even the feared Widow will try to flee
rather than attack, like any small creature
with common sense when confronted
by a larger one. Or they curl up and
play dead. Only as a last resort will
Widows bite and even then, reported
fatalities are usually fake news.

Indeed, if she were a Black Lace-Weaver,
the tables will eventually be turned as she
becomes the victim of her many hatchlings
who will actively devour her.
There's a video.

Last night I wanted to drape a cloth
over my host's full-length bathroom
mirror, but this morning is another day.

I have the body I now have.
So does last night's spider with her
large, fertile abdomen, which may soon,
depending on who she really is,
become the death of her.

                                        2017

Eleusinian string theory of grief

life bubbles up from darkness
a loom each day restrung

you turned the jagged edges
of her death over and over
poems twisting onto the spindle of
your grief no one else could handle

but from that spinning
came new life not
as one might think but
as permission

to take grieving's
absolute and through its eye
to drop the shuttle even farther
down to find there is

no finality from which
the hopelessness of death
cannot someday recover
no atom of despair

that cannot be untwined
into quivering strings
hummed and plucked
remembered and woven

the calm courage
of those initiates
who over and over danced

a fervent loop into the very stone
around the fissure into which she fell

ca. 1995

41

where the gulls go

like arrows
hundreds cross

at dusk
the line

between land
and lake

with no
hesitation no

quiver they
fly straight

into dark
mist invisible

even before
reaching horizon

knowing exactly where
they are going

and why

1997

Redwings

Unprecedented, they are back
before my birthday this year,
raw and raucous, staking claims
along Lake Michigan's bank.

Cheer-eee the males call, show-offs
swaying reckless atop slim reeds,
gripping cattails dipping
wildly with their buoyant weight.

But it seems this spring
has landed too soon and I fear
perhaps our blue planet, that huge
unwatched pot, has begun to simmer

with our clustered heat, so the spell
of winter's crystal cold
might melt for good before
great-grandchildren can play, mittened, in snow.

But today the sun calms and warms
the pallor of my worried
scrunched-up northern face.
In a week my birthday

will come bounding round the corner
like an old dog joyously sniffing spring,
not wanting to exhale, so abundant
the intoxicating scents.

2000

Wild Rhubarb

—for Malala Yousafzai

A year into the wilderness of puberty
a girl in Kansas vowed to strive
for perfection in all things.

The backyard's smooth expanse of grass
stretched flawless save
for one large weed in the center.

So one day she knelt,
pulled off the weed's long leaves,
which wasn't hard. But then

she saw the wrist-thick,
yellow cord plugged deep
into the hard prairie clay.

Had she been younger,
she might have thought
she was digging to the other

side of Earth, but
her growing brain no longer
harbored such beliefs.

But had she been more attuned
that day, she might have felt
her trowel recoil from the shots

in a Pakistani school bus, might have
screamed with the other girls, as one
just her age was gunned down for learning.

She might have felt the rage
of millions of stunned women
whose perfect girls

were married at eight,
refused the right to study,
stunted behind the burqa:

might have felt stirrings of rage
at those, some in *her state,*
who sought, from behind the Cross,

to control the fertility of girls.
As she dug she was learning something
about the strength of determination,

something about the deep
roots of imperfection, yet it was still
too early to tell how

things that seem to submit,
leaves never allowed
to gather light, will still

hunker, vestigial stems, and through
the thickest matter, put forth even
thicker, even greener shoots.

2013

On the 50th Anniversary of Brown v. the Board of Education

On May 17, 1954, the U.S. Supreme Court ended federally sanctioned racial segregation in the public schools.

Then, children with straightened hair and shined
shoes glanced back dazed by the flash bulbs

as they stepped through the battered-down door.
Today, their great-grandsons in baggy

pants saunter into the room with practiced
meanness to show how tough they are

or hunch in huge Air Jordans,
earphones dangling round their necks, the first

day in your college English class. They flirt
with the girl at the next desk, glance at you

with dark hooded eyes that reveal nothing.
Taunted by friends as 'white' for being here,

they mask their doubt that maybe they don't belong,
that canons and computers contain a code

too alien to learn. Before indentured
evenings with the basketball team,

some write essays about the alleys behind
their homes, about a child and a homeless man

making a game of finding cans
to stuff in a dirty net. Or about a southern

city where a neighbor called their mama
if they really messed up.

They touch you on the shoulder only after
they have failed, to tell you that they don't

blame you. And even if they cheat,
that too, is not because of you: it's that

they didn't want to disappoint.
When over Thanksgiving a street brother,

on the street, a brother is pulled, pulled
from his driver's seat and shot, he is shot

right in front of his brother, who, in your class
has begun, whose writing begins, to blaze,

who, when he leaves, when he leaves your office
after touching your shoulder, telling you why

he's stopped coming, stopped coming so
close, so close, to the end, leaving your office

he flashes a look over his shoulder, glances
back, pen zipped in his jacket like a gun.

                                                        2005

47

Rescue

*We hold hard to those we love even as they die away from us
and we continue to pursue them, through dreams, into poems.*
—Maxine Kumin

My daughter said she dreamed
she had set fire
to her childhood home,
the house we still live in,
then kept running back to save
all the most valuable things.

Once dreams flooded my nights and I
would flounder after them, rescuing as many
as my young memory could
from the torrents of Lethe, stilling the shimmer
of them in my mind by force of will,
wringing them out, spreading
their delicate tissues to dry,
to decipher on daylight's lined paper.

Today the Walgreens clerk's daughter,
her beauty in combat camouflage, smiles up
at us from her golden frame by the register.

In Iraq? my daughter asks.
Was, is the answer.
Killed in '07.

Her mother and I trade hooded glances.
I can see she fears forgetting already
that smile,
the fragments of that final day,
her daughter deployed, leaving
home and, at the last minute, turning,
retrieving from her childhood home
some cherished talisman to take to war.

2011

The Self-Organizing Universal Nail Salon

As the young, slight, male manicurist
deftly massages my hand, we turn our heads
in opposite directions as if such pleasure
between strangers were unseemly, in light

of everyday suffering. But who am I
to believe that broken things might not
even now be making their way toward
new, if temporary, wholes: the ragged

edges of extremities healed, soothed,
polished by the practiced touch of water
on pitted rock, by the ecstatic surrender
of stone to the repeated plunging of wave?

2017

thorny devil

—after George Herbert's "The Flower"

thorny devil
crawls in desert
down under

six-inch lizard
eater of ants
looking fiercer

than it really is
when faced with
what it fears—

its would-be killer
bites off its false head
real head bent

between knees
thorns protruding
everywhere

so far it already
reminds me
of myself

but this most:

tiny labyrinthine
channels on its skin
conduct the little

water at hand
right to the corners
of its mouth:

just so when i
resist, too
dumb to drink,

do life's
close passages
feed the precise

fluidity i need
to my fixed and dust-dry
lips: blessed and centered,

graced but unaware

                                    2000–2003

Descent

A warbler cries out as I cut
seed-empty sunflowers, shears
hacking through hollow stems.

Last year they scattered wild
over the garden:
so many tangled at the end
they had to be tied
together, lurching across
straitjackets of twine.

I toss them
into a rotting pile.

There is no promise
of anything beyond,
of such a dream
as green motion.

I hear the warbler cry.
The thin yellow feathers
of her flowers have withered.

Even more tender things will be lost
in first frost.

I cover red roses checked
mid-bud.

The moment approaches absolute—
a burial,
a grief,
a sadness in the midst
of rest.

The dirt under my nails
cries out for ritual.

I clear closets,
strip paint from doors,
unhook curtains,
rumple beds,
snarl my hair,
scatter notes, lists,
my things to do,
unbutton and unbuckle,
kick off shoes,

swivel upside down
and dangle
in this wild, bared
garden listening to all the cries etched
at the ends of things.

                                                    1998

Even in January

Holidays over, we step into stillness.
Today there's rain.
Muddy fields lie fallow, open to the sky.
Pools settle in hollows, littered with seed.

Freed from the city, I come with my dog
who, shivering with joy,
crashes through damp leaves,
bounds over fallen branches,
snuffles soggy bark.
Ahead, she stands panting
on the nearest mound.

Grey light and mist swell,
deepening green moss to emerald,
turning yellow stubble left in fields to gold,
but softening others:

pale pumpkins—deflated balloons—
twist free from withered stalks;
red winterberry's haze masks
smoke-dense distant trees.

My socks are wet; toes numb.

Great curves sweep across the land.
A crow takes flight on black taffeta wings.

1993

without desire

sickness has sifted like silt
into the flow
of your summer

that old nemesis claiming
a visit or maybe
a home

either way he will filch
your delight in food,
beauty, laughter, movement,

show you how loosely
your silken senses tie you
to life

how finicky your taste
how jarring touch
how heavily

sound and smell intrude
as your body slakes even
minimal motion

sight remains a draw
but he will render
it distant as

the out of doors you are missing
lying with him in your
hot twisted bed

tv athletes seem another species
from the viewing box
of pain

dependence becomes a bore as others demand
you kick the bastard out,
better get better soon

outside life like a Greek shade
you watch its smoky richness
without desire

gourmet fare no longer tempts,
beauty no longer beckons,
urgent tasks no longer summon

and the morning you wake
without his arms flung
over you

and feel a flick of craving
to rise, eat, talk,
you shiver, hesitate,

wonder why you should again edge out
onto those flimsy surfaces
and when, not

if, your departed lover
who's left, as usual, a mess
will return to stay.

2001

Fallow

Somewhere near that blur
between summer and fall, the dog,

parentage uncertain, and I
stray to a field left untilled,

filled with sharp grass grown
jointed and tall.

Outside the rim of tractor ruts,
an oak of some age drops smooth

perfect acorns in dry dust.
Were I an oak, only now

would I be old enough
to drop seed.

I sit on a stone surrounded
by feral grass and listen

to the loud whispers of its
uneasy dead. Small hoppers

and paired yellow butterflies
share a separate silence.

Remnants of corn, clover, soybeans
ring the field. The dog

pants in the warm, off-center sun.
For the moment we sit

easy on our haunches, not needing,
at least not needing to know, for now,

exactly where we are.

1995–2021

Twilight Flight

Trailing the cusp of dark for hours, sun never quite
setting, I float in a pod of timelessness, far

from the frazzle of airport malls hawking illusions
of permanence to passengers perpetually in between.

Seven miles over the dotted lights of nameless cities I might find
on maps, I trace reflected ribbons of still rivers flowing south

as we slant northwest over hills lidded with dusk.
Loose discs of cloud drift, lily pads on the membrane

of a vast pond, obscuring what lies rooted in the mud below.
Like the red sandstone desert we once drove through,

empty mist mirrors the encrimsoned sun just now sunk
beneath the verge of world.

Then the first flash of lightning quickens, leaps nimbly
as a nightbird's cry—to yet another limb.

How can one see all this and live? Those around me doze,
whisper, restless in this cavity, confined.

Soon, hurtling through flashing space, we fall toward the world.
Time rushes back, rivulets peel across my tiny window.

Sun set at last, night finally born after long labor,
I roll myself and all my baggage home.

2000–2023

Part Two: A Question of Art

Sheherazade on the Streets

> *. . . expect truth only from [she] whose belly is full.*
>   —Lewis Hyde's *Trickster Makes this World*

Stories can save your life.

She began with what she could tell
from my face and dress and hurry
I most wanted to hear:
Lady, I ain't askin' for nuthin.'

Neither old nor young, fat nor thin,
black nor white, she perched on
the edge of a stone planter by the Walgreens'
snow-banked lot. Five pm,
and tears were streaming down her cheeks.

> *I ain't askin' for nuthin',*
> she went on, *but I just*
> *can't take the cold no more.*
> *Cops can't do nuthin' for me*
> *'cause I am sober. Gave me*
> *a breathylizer.*
> *If I was drunk they would have took me in*
> *out of the cold. I be lookin'*
> *to trade the rest of my food stamps for*
> *27 dollars to buy a bed*
> *for the week, someone told me 'bout.*
> *I call the shelters on my 'bama phone*
> *every night but I'm 26th*
> *on the list. They turnin' away*
> *every single woman in this cold.*

She rocked back and forth, not looking
me in the eye. It was ten
degrees of meanness out there with
a killing wind. I didn't need food
stamps, but intrigued, I scurried back
to the Walgreens' ATM,
which quickly spit out 40 bucks.

Where is this place? I asked.
I'll show you, she said,
jumping right into my car.

> *My mother and me, we used to live in*
> *my grandfather's house. He was a preacher*
> *and 'cause of that his property tax was put*
> *on hold. But when he died they finally come due*
> *but my mother, she couldn't pay.*
> *After she died I was tossed out on the street.*
> *A neighbor took me in for a while to mind*
> *her kids but when her man came home from jail*
> *he took one look and kicked me right out.*
> *I been sleeping in doorways ever since.*
> *One thousand and one hard nights.*

This here the ghetto, she gestured like a guide
as we neared the old house with a sagging porch
she readily pointed out. We hugged.

I asked her name and she told me. I told her mine.
I watched her dart up the stairs, then drove away.

After just one wakeful night of listening
to the evil portents of the wind, I threw back
my warm covers, drove again to the ATM,
punched out five more twenties and
easily wound my way back
to the *ghetto,* this time crossing
a no longer perceptible line.
She was huddled on a broken-down
dirty couch in that cold house
watching a blaring TV. Wrapped up
in all her raggedy clothes, she said
my room's upstairs, but
I'm worried 'bout what I'll do
when this week is up.

Happily, I presented her with
the twenties and my cell phone number.
She smiled. We hugged again.

Back home, my people shook their heads.
told me I'd been scammed;
a reporter I called said this woman
was well-known for her stories.
Change your phone number, she advised.
Give her no more money.

And so I did, and I did not.
But I'll tell you this:

Like all great storytellers who subsist
on that bare thread between harsh truth
and the sweet recompense of fiction,
she charmed me, made me believe
every single word and changed me
in the telling. I still wonder
what will happen next.

Whenever Sheherazade comes to spin
her tales, hoard every nugget of your gullibility,
let your hurry, for a moment, fall away,
wrap yourself snug in what she's woven
out of whole cloth, perhaps even pay
a little something toward the royalties
that are, no doubt, her due.

ca. 2012

A Question of Art

While Argerich plays Prokofiev, I sit
in one of the cheapest front seats, see
only her hands, her feet, lifting, falling, feel
the thrum of troops marching in Russia
in 1917 but also the sweetness of youth:
hope and brash dissonance form a ready background
to my grief.

She takes me deeply into it then out
the other side, so when the sonata ends—
that iteration of it—when there remained beats
of silence before she lowers her hands and rises
to face the chaos of applause, I can surrender
sorrow to that silence and move
at least a measure closer to acceptance,
and am comforted, like that

Northern Irish hostage in Beirut forty winters
ago, chained to a wall, beaten and cold,
who received an orange on what must have been
a Christmas morning, who did not eat it even
though he knew that in a few days it must shrivel. But
before that happened, he could give himself over
to an orb of color packed tight with promise in that den
of death, hooking on, maybe, to that beat of silence
just before the orange began to shrink
back into the surrounding cacophony of pain.

As I reach for my keys and coat to leave the hall,
I imagine Keats, twenty-three—lungs already hostage
to the bacillus that would kill him two years on—
staring at that empty, ancient Grecian urn,
painted with an innocent heifer garlanded,
forever led to sacrifice, and I wonder, did Keats
really hold that urn, warm it with his hands before reaching
for his pen, latching on to that silence and stretching it,
riding it full tilt so that he might drink
from its pure source forever?

2018–2023

The Craft

The lyf so short, the craft so long to lerne.
—Chaucer

Meaning arrives slowly,
a song from great distance,
a breeze
passing over ditch water.
While it lasts, you lean
into its shiver.

You do not master a craft;
it brushes you with surprise.
And if you tender the tips of
your most hopeless longing,
your most stubborn faults,

craft will bind them into a beauty so
dense, so pure, so rare, so common, you
will find yourself cast into a spell of amazement,
of gratitude so deep you will feel
forever young in its thrall.

You do not master a craft;
you are the village fool that fumbles,
falls, breaks the cask:
then frees, attends, willingly surrenders
to the genie everything you have and are—

your seed, your root, your core, your
insatiable need.

2012–2014

67

Sonata

i. exposition

This is about a girl at the piano.

This is about flight.
This is about practice.
This is about the practice that makes possible
the flight.

This is about beginning, the first
part of the pattern when it seems
you can do anything,
take any form:

first stroke on canvas,
first kiss, first caress of a chord.

This is about the possibilities
of small hands.

> Daughter of my body, you sit rigid
> before the keyboard, balking at what
> it requires of you.

> Haltingly, you try a melody,
> slump, correct a wrong note, sigh.

A cripple came to me in my dream,
perhaps my crippled sister's dream,
trying to keep up, demanding my love.
I wanted only to be free.

The music perches on the rack
like air before a flight,
the keys grounded before me like
planes in a port.

You begin.

ii. development

> Daughter of my spirit,
> I feel your hands grow excited,
> sensitive, quiver
> with unsung music.

So it was for me when our house,
saddened by my sister's death,
permitted no dance.

Seated, stilled, except for my hands,
like my sister's bird-like fingers
fluttering in an iron lung,
no one knew how we flew
over the grave of death.

I lugged my yellow books
to the teacher's house after school
where she recognized
at once what no one else had seen:
my love of flight and
my lack of control. She hooked
me by the back of my vision,
made me account for carelessness.

Made me slow down.
Made me lumber through exercises
invented by men so old
I never knew
their faces.

> I sat rigid
> before the keyboard,
> balking at what
> it required of me.

Over and over, trying
to get it right, at last
there came moments when even
the most difficult arpeggios
spun out like silk from fingertips,
when playing was like wings
effortlessly brushing bells:

two hands in consort, soaring
through a forest of intricate harmonies,
not caring for the names
of notes, not needing me, really,
at all, except to get out of their way.

iii. recapitulation

Then there are times when
fingers are stiff wooden
clubs translating nothing.

Playing for a lover,
wanting him to hear the very
best of me, of the music, my fingers
playing on the keys as they play on his
body, but, faltering,

failing, falling, him not hearing,
him turning away to make a call.

So it was when I panicked
at recital, like a dream in which
I can't remember the way home,
the swift flight of fingers
crashing to earth,
creatures that never
knew how to dance.

Daughter of my heart, you sit
rigid before the keyboard, balking
at what it requires of you.

I too have stamped my foot at God,
demanding respite, seeing no progress,
pleading for release.

So was your pregnancy:
a huge helplessness
before the creation
of someone else.
Limitation and failure and waiting:
time and space and size were
barriers to the ultrasound of
boundless music.

When you were small
I did not play at all.

Dust sifted between keys,
which you tentatively touched
with sticky jam.

Secretly gardening, I
cultivated beauty, hoarded
landscapes improvised
rock by rock,
seed by seed,
note by unheard note.

Now I understand
when you want to shut the door,
grow incensed when I sing along.

iv. coda

Melodies remain; words fade.

I remember love: the faces
of my sister, who also played,
and of others I have also loved
grow dim.

> Daughter of my soul,
> at last understanding imperfection,
> honoring the best we can do
> done over and over until
> we throw off crutches,
> surpass ourselves, leaving earth,
> unaware.

> Now am I lost in play while you
> cup hands and shout at me while
> pots boil over.

A woman, playing
alone, composes
herself, knowing
there is always more
to draw upon.

Early death, late
bloom, make no difference.

Space, and time, and
limitation, and failure,
are means.

To see that truth
is to see
the gate in the wall,
sequel, reassurance
there is yet more,
like flight,
to pull from impossibility,
from inaudible frequencies,
into the reach
of real.

2000–2010

Palimpsest: Painting Her Again

I keep scraping the canvas / And painting him over again /
But he keeps slipping away.

—Edward Hirsch

Putting her fragments
Together in yet
Another way

Turning her differently-aged
Profiles this way and that
So as to see new things

In different lights
Even though the outcome
Is always the same

Putting her repeated death
Against once-future events
Casting it into differing perspectives

The cherished nieces
Arriving years after
The fact of loss

Connecting her to a whole
World of living relations
Memories

Shaded with deepening insight
Never-before-seen colors added
To my basic box of crayons

Foreshortening my grief
Triangulating its source
As I scribble wax over oil

Still trying to get
A fix
On sorrow

2015

Jimbo's Car Wash

When her husband died, a friend asked you
where to get her car washed. Happy to help
with something so easy, you told her
go to Jimbo's, get the 'silver' wash—
the best deal. And tip big.

And she did. For years, her car gleamed.

At Jimbo's there was always a long, patient
line of salt-encrusted cars needing loving care.
When it came your turn, two quick, friendly
workers vacuumed the floor mats and seats,
discarded your trash, then guided you onto the rails.

Sudsy brushes caressed your cranky car;
there was a spurt of wax you could buy
for an extra buck. Four laughing, joking workers
were always waiting as you emerged.
They would snap to work rubbing you down
with clean towels, outside, then tenderly
washing the inside windows, wiping out the dirty
rubber cup that held your coffee and spare change.

You would roll out feeling clean,
shining, renewed.

It was an art.

Then, one night, Jimbo's vanished—
razed to the ground. Demolished.
Just bare earth, not even rubble.
No fence, no forwarding address.

You were stunned—couldn't take it in,
felt angry out of all proportion.

Today you're told your friend
has a fast-moving cancer, and the feeling
roars back: the futile *why*
hurtling through every abrupt
annihilation of all you've ever loved but never
imagined would ever
actually die.

2023

dry spell

time pools in the copper pocket of afternoon as
you step out onto the suspension bridge
solid ground coming and going

you grip the rope, trying to steady as you inch

your way across and away
from what you'd decided to say
toward words that might or might not come

ca. 2012

Resistance

Haven't touched the piano all summer
everyone sleeps so late, and later there
is never time: noise proliferates.

Atop the sticky, unpolished mahogany, the composer
lies in state, unmediated, un-divined,
broken circuit in the damp, limp

stack of music I avoid riffling,
for when I hinge open the cover of the keys
all will have fallen to pieces, the fugue

so carefully fingered in fall, brought up painstakingly
to tempo in spring, this child gone haywire, unruly
through neglect, will have slipped out of my hand.

House proud, my father knew how quickly
all comes to disarray. Years
after his death, on a trip from another state,

on impulse I drove past what was our house
to stare at rusted awnings, blistered paint,
rooms packed with rowdiness, lawn

littered with beer bottles, paper, trash.
Meticulous, he was: mended phone wires,
spiking up rough poles in prairie blizzards,

later laid his toughened hands to the mysteries
of shortwave, microwave, radio, satellite,
his mouth filling with more and more

and more magical words: conductor, frequency,
transformer, resistor, alternator. He was abstracted,
yet he made things work, the diagrams of circuits

carefully drawn in our cool basement—something
like the dotted scores I struggled to read, sweating
in the heat upstairs. Eventually I saw how

starting takes the most energy: to budge from zero,
to decide to choose to let oneself be moved,
how inattention cripples energy or makes it run

after you, amok, yet how utterly
essential measured resistance is
to flow and serendipity.

The composer's blocked current, intensely still,
holds fire while I choose to charm my monsters,
make deliberate descent, close the circuit

like a door behind us, and let my wayward hands,
fluttering neither back nor forward,
lead us back, here, to limping, fecund time.

2002

cadenza

understanding is not the essential thing

(the careful pattern in temporary sand)

life goes on without it

           unpunctuated.

within sky   clouds compose

water and stone   arrange themselves   on the floor of the forest

hearts go on loving   beating

                 rhythms

     without measure or conductor

the smooth egg of our life   slips free   from

the score's crumpled shell;

             anything

we don't control seems a miracle

sight-reading robs us of invention

       scripts cheat us of surprise   (spurs of the moment)

       variations of impulse

          provisional improvisation

            epiphanies of providence

               the unrepeatability of

our own cadences

           fall

      be   tween

the lines   of the canon.

            ca. 1998

80

For Pianist Mitsuko Uchida

All the moments
of her life so far
have led to this:

to sculpt the silence
between two notes
by Webern:

to enrapture time,
to entice time's
physical body

into this hollowed eddy,
this dappled net,
a full-fleshed fish—

spelled and stroked—
stroked and spelled—

then yielded back
into the rapids,

the rushing din
of undifferentiated
nows.

2010

Delicate Instruments

Pianos are delicate instruments that do not endure forever.
                                              —Sophie Pinkham

I play a century-old, massive instrument
savagely constructed from elephant tusks and catgut,
the heartwood of old-growth spruce.

It was built four years before the Titanic's piano shattered
on the North Atlantic floor, its keys, felts, hinges rising like
ghosts freed from bolts holding down the wood—
dried, bent, and glued by Steinway Village workers
crossing picket lines.

The upper octaves have gone quite flat, clamoring
for new pins and hammers I can't afford.

Everywhere I see mutilated sounding boards discarded on curbs.

These days, ever out of kilter, I practice, needing to soothe
an anxious brain with ever-changing patterns and designs,
fugues and variations.

Each night my mind replays the Bach C- toccata my fingers
struggle to learn by day, tripping over themselves to make space
for the joyful notes pressing themselves into memory, into
the soft loops of my delicate, my feral, my pacing
human brain.

2020

'Round Midnight

REM cycle i:

Step out of the body
for a little minute, having
worked all day to earn

this right; step out
of the score for an instant;
stand up and play your

fluid truth. Improvise:
fill the silence, the space left
for you and your solo,

constructed and construed in that fine
pandemonium of the moment.
Become the spindle for those nets of notes

swaying round you, for those
whose sleeping bodies dance to your pulse.
Thelonius Sphere Monk and Johann

Sebastian Bach lean out of their shadows
watching, listening, tapping their slippered feet,
you the one stepping up, now,

you the one in the spotlight,
the whorl of your fingerprints
on the keys, the snip of your

DNA in the mix,
dissonance and silences
honored within the math and

intricate physics of music,
keeping the devil on edge,
keeping sadness at bay.

waking cycle i:

Today you read that cancer is a riff
on the body's cells: the daughter cells,
the daughters of the daughter cells
into which a malignance sings its repeated
aria, independent
of the group, the agreed-upon
structure, and will not
sit down but keeps on
playing, perseverating, far
after everyone else has
stopped listening, gone home.

REM cycle ii:

A flowing flock of dark starlings poises
to tip, stretches like a rubber band,
then suddenly shifts, noiseless,
darting together, diving, fanning out

onto the stage of this unfastening minute
where also creeps the ad-libbing world,
demolishing the limit
of what we thought was possible, uncurling.

At night, colored surfaces are dull.
How do birds and squirrels survive such cold?
You keep the feeders full.
The owls that kill and rats that scrounge are bold.

Surprise encircles our little selves.
The rhyme comes out of nowhere, as it were,
as if the poem were made by elves
though, in a quantum field, there is only blur.

waking cycle ii:

You pull remnants of the dream
'round you, watch the sun come,
without haste or fear, to this cold
day to light up the morning
urgencies of every wild
creature: to eat and drink,
to frolic and be free of malady.

The dreaming tortoise of time
covers us all with its crazed shell,
protects the genesis of melody,
dance, poetry, and
the murmurations of starlings,
keeps sadness at bay.
You roll out of bed, barefoot
in your cold kitchen, drink your coffee,
watch bird by awkward bird
land on the line of your ledge,
fiercely strut, squawk,
await impatiently its rightful place
at the day's funnel of seed.

The piano calls you, again,
to solitary practice and today's
precious measure of mistakes.

2014–2023

The Yang and the Yin of Poetry

i. Yang

There is a power in poetry
of air and fire:
wordsmith welding worlds
in the crucible of metaphor.

Cold, words jangle against
each other: hot, they link
like magician's hoops.
Molecules of words whizz,
readying for the
join
like skaters racing over ice
before they jump,
skiers gaining speed before they leap
over the edge,

dancing to ecstasy,
falling in love,
chanting till glib meaning blurs
to a cone of power,
a sharp point of sun
smoldering through paper.

Poets should wear welders' helmets,
goggles, weave tight circles
of make-believe white light
around their work as
protection against
madness,
burning out,
letting it slip
away.

ii. Yin

There is also a power of
stillness,
gravity,
time:

snow finally slipping
from a branch,

age tenderly
unbuttoning
the body like
a mother
undressing a child
so spirit may
breathe.

There is power
in the patient receptivity of rocks,
each fitting to the next
or tossed by a wave
as in the game of Statue—
each holding position,
remaining until
we all see
and call its name.

There is a power in giving up,
surrender, loyalty to limitations,
the levels to which we fall.

There is a power of time,
drawing things out
to the full:
the same obstacle
again and
again,

the grace of a long-sought
answer after sleep,

effortless words
sliding silently into place.

ca. 1992

directions for playing

life should be lived legato and
rock climbing sure as hell better
be legato for there is danger
leaving the ground on your own
and swimming is legato only because of
water which is very legato but not so much
as smooth crystal-linked ice or as staccato
as rain beginning to pelt your head
                              learning anything
including how to be married is staccato at first though
the goal is legato but that takes practice which hopefully
will stitch together the staccatos and draw
them tight to the point where the strokes
are not even seen beneath the surface or
in the seam
                there are those who stumble
up the stairs to enlightenment young and never
look down and those who take to water as babes and can't
remember when they knew anything but
legato, *exempli grati:*
                        the woman in the next lane with her smooth
enjambment between laps surely is legato—one who started
swimming when wet behind the ears long after polio left its jagged
    blip
on the surface of some historical pool but for me learning legato
has been a life of sitting anxious on the edge and wanting it badly
enough to be willing to die if need be while slapping
together staccatos—hit or miss—mostly not getting it right
rising and indeed plunging but not in a good way though
my crawl finally cobbled together a quasi-legato—a compromise
of air and water that has got me eventually to the end
                                        and in the end

maybe it's not what we do ourselves to connect
just life sooner or later tired of itself as separate
staccato particles rises then falls readily back into waves of legato
like that magician's trick of stuffing scarf after scarf into a
fist then smiling and teasing out billows of gracefully knotted silk
or faceless paper-dolls with just the tiniest point of join

2013

Prima Materia

Out of the imperfect mess of our lives,
out of the prison of our self-pity,
the mundane drivel of our minds,

out of the glacial movement of time,
the dirt we can never clean completely
off the windowsill or pry out
from under our fingernails,
through the slimy remains of last
year's garden,

through our stubbornness,
despite our resistance,
the acid screams of our fear and
the greed of our desire—

through all this arises a force
so confident, so vast
that we ride it unaware,
a huge beloved animal that knows
its way home.

When we try to command it with
our tiny feet and whips,
or abandon it miles from home, hoping
it will never find its way back,
nevertheless, it will return, like life
embedded in a rhizome.

Ugly, unkempt, twisted, dry,
it will wend its way back
to our door,
where it will curl up and wait
to be admitted,
watered,
known,
loved.

1994

On Her Holy Outskirts of Theory

But actual music is always more complicated and subtle
than the charts that try to explain it.
                              —William Duckworth

In theory, time could run backwards.
In theory, everybody could live indefinitely.
Every rocket would launch.
Both wave and particle could be tracked.
Rabbits would not eat my tulip buds.
In rabbit theory, there would be no repellant.

We've cross-stitched oxymorons and conditionals onto samplers,
into the garment of grammar with acknowledgement of exceptions,
whip-stitched the lingo of wishful surprise
into hems on the outskirts of theory.

But lingua franca is filled with the familiar present-tense verbs,
        infinitives,
practical paper patterns pinned to the usual cloth.

But new bolts occasionally unroll: this year's feathered, striped
        tulip replaces the plain purple;
a new riff or cadenza shifts the common song;
the dictionary swells by a single word.

Trapped jokers from time-to-time escape through some quirk or
        anomaly, some loophole of desire, through knotty questions like
        why
or why not?

Lady of limits and limitlessness,
of laughter and theoretical music,
nameless be thy name.

May visions come, desires be done,
on flowered earth, outside of heaven.
Give hungry creatures untheoretical food,
loosen our theories as we let our seams out
to allow for dissonance.
Lead us fools into temptation.
Deliver us from the theories of evil,
for folded into thy hems,
sown into the furrowed seems of
the blind-stitched outskirts lurk
renewal and possibility for
ever, forever,
and ever,
more.

ca. 2014

Heart Rest

i.

Perhaps begin, like Mohammed,
called to prayer five times a day;

turn toward what's always there
on the backside of your business:

alternating at first, slowly,
heart rest with heart beat,

the silver side of waves,
the concave so akin to convex

you think it one:

the back behind every front,
the shadow of light there, even in darkness.

Lay beats of silence around the familiar,
bracket absorption in the quotidian.

Later, having come to perceive space,
perhaps you will see angels,

will pray ceaselessly,
float on hidden wings.

Possibly you will compose with rests,
rather than wooden notes.

Cage 4'33" of silence,*
but even an

eighth,

a sixteenth,

94

a thirty-second, even the tiniest rest
gives pause,

enables you to hear

the change
just after a poem,

the echo just before
a baby cries.

ii.

Space lives, felt but feared,
a wild animal at the edge of sight
in a lair of little deaths through which breath
comes and goes.

It lives between notes,
in a round of imperfect fifths,
hidden, the darkness between
frames of film,
the necessary emptiness
between spokes that blur
faster and faster into great
moveable wheels
on which we might balance,
water on which we could walk.

It dwells in the implausible distance
between the atoms of our very bodies
we think so solid, barriers that seem
as impenetrable as mountains but through which
we could move could we find passage.

The rest may be what remains,
the liminal between seasons,
dusk, dawn,
skin winding off a snake
slipping between worlds.

The scaffold comes down,
the safety net and rules.

What remains is the rest,
freed, potent,
the silence of risk
within utter safety,
a cup brimming with hollow,
a smiling mime pointing toward
the impossible, a fool
dancing across emptiness.

1994

* reference to composer John Cage's work *Four Minutes and Thirty-three Seconds* (1952), in which the performer(s) remain utterly silent onstage for that amount of time.

The Art of Working the Bases

Alone for a week, I don't think as much
about you as I thought I would.

Back home, lurching around the bases
of our marriage, I believe that twenty years

seems a haven to strive for, within
reach. Battered, with stained uniforms,

we sign secret code to each other.
At times we have both been ready to head

for the showers. But something hangs on,
maybe some days no more than that

you know exactly where to scratch
the itchy spot on my sweaty back.

The children we were stare at us from frames
on the wall in the company of our own children.

Hooting in bleachers, eating popcorn, they want
to see how this all ends.

Between this and the next line I write
is a chasm of whiteness I must somehow bridge.

Caught between second and third, I laugh, prance,
act the fool, slide, give it my damndest.

2003–2023

She Watches Her Hands

She watches them minister to each other
before she sleeps, one rubbing lotion
into the scar on the back of the other
at the end of the day before arranging themselves
at her side or folding as one in Namaste
between her thighs or under the pillow.

In her dream they gossip, embolden each other,
perhaps through their tiny ganglia,
whisper to themselves like joyful children
who have not yet conceived of otherness.

In some alien magnitude of wilderness
about which she knows nothing, they rehearse
tomorrow's C# arpeggio over and over
without complaint; practice catching the water glass
that will next day fall out of the cupboard, together
cupping it—just as a baseball catcher's hands frame strikes—
the second before it would have shattered across the floor.

2020

Part Three: A Question of Time

Quivira

1541:

Coronado rides in on horseback
looking for a legendary city of
gold, but finds only

a flow of grasshopper, turkey, deer,
migrating birds, sand, salt,
and savages in

moveable thatched huts, following bison.
Disappointed, he still names it *Quivira*
before returning to Spain.

1875:

Kiowa watch from lookouts while buffalo,
shot as vermin, topple to the earth
to rot where they fall,

skeletons so thick you can step one
to the other. Nothing turns, nothing
transforms. Stacked bones

mark the trackless prairie for schooners whose
dust Satanta, hidden in sandhills and tall
bluestem grass, marks.

Around one mound of bones—an
imaginary center—rises a town:
a sod hotel, one room to let,

blacksmith, a bank. Forts crop up against
Satanta, the Osage, Wichita, the Kansa,
scalp locks designating their bands:

Sky and Earth peoples, north and south, they
master seven stages of sacred knowledge, dream
dreams replete with

spirit of tree, sun, light, dark
painted on their shields, foretelling
a bleak future.

Because buffalo fed the Indian, hunters
wipe out the southern herd by '74,
Sheridan's winter campaign,

his Red River War. Other vermin
blocking the plow are destroyed for bounties:
dens of rattlers, prairie dogs,

the coyotes and jackrabbits my father still
kills forty years later. Onto the now
nearly empty prairie

steps the farmer who traces off claims
with a wagon wheel, broadcasts wheat
by hand, harvests

with cradle and scythe (sickle for the old
buffalo wallows and salt marshes),
grain threshed by cattle

or tossed in the air to blow away chaff.
Snake sticks line the walls of churches
bricked from red clay.

A few frame farm houses rise
from sacred cottonwood and willow. Women
share root-stalk

starts of roses hauled from Missouri, quilt,
preserve what they can, fear the Kiowa
who sometimes steal

them and their children, hate the prostitute
who steals their husbands. One night they march
her by the arm

to the depot, north end of town,
pay her exorbitant fare, push her
onto the train east,

along with a hundred cars of lucrative hides.
Most farmers endure until the drought
of '80, begetting poverty,

prairie fires, blizzards, tornados, typhoid,
snake bite, grasshoppers, nerves ratcheted up
by the south wind

that never ceases—by loneliness, silence, wished-for
music, pined for shelter of trees. The turtles
find no water,

the silent trout curl up. The sheet water
of wells sinks from sight; wallows dry,
crack, fill with sand.

Feathered lances drip blood; Satanta
leaps to death from the penitentiary,
is buried deep without

paint, sacred bark or buffalo robes,
rocks, food, bow and arrow, pipe
or extra clothing.

Without proper ceremony, his skin
does not fall cleanly away
from his bones.

1945:

In the elevator south of town,
out by the other railroad tracks, across
the cracked tarmac

the old, angled sidewalk bricks break,
sink into sand, the stored wheat settles,
the gold weight of it

falling to mold, falling to mildew save
for the constant thrum of a giant blower all
night all day

swirling the gathered grain, stirring, separating,
swirling, stirring, separating, within the closed
moist knuckles of

the elevator, whirling the clean grain
mounding in its concrete cup,
while a mile away

fungus visits three small graves
in less than a year; three small
cages of bone take longer

than flinted arrowheads to flake
away. Grain in the field sinks
to earth not to root

but to rot; spores, smuts, nothing
turns, nothing transforms—*fusarium, astilago
nuda, parasitic phytophthora.*

What is planted does not grow.
Wombs leak. Sperm does not engender.
Hope wanes.

I was conceived, it was whispered,
on the bank of the Rattlesnake
River, winding through

this reserve where my parents slept
on army cots under canvas
or, I hope, under

the bare sky where the lavish summer
constellations whirl: Lyra, given
by Apollo to Orpheus,

poet and musician, rising late
on the horizon. As he might say,
I leapt into the cup

of my mother's womb, stopped its mouth,
began to weave my cage of bones.
For once, hope

did not die like a runt bounding
heedless from the dusty bed of a pickup.
Yet not being

born stolid and single-minded,
I was ever destined
to disappoint.

1975:

My grandfather dies of cancer.
By his empty farmhouse
spring lilacs and lilies.

Busted farms are sold or taken over.
Farm Bureaus become conglomerates,
the latest

company store feeding on debt, offering
new weapons to eradicate new
vermin: pesticides,

anti-fungals, antibiotics, weed
killers. Atrazine contaminates
ground water.

Cancer appears in young families who pack
up and leave the cemetery where
a teddy bear swings like

a lynching over a grave. Growth hormones,
stimulants: rampant animals, deceptive
hollow lushness of wheat.

Refinery polluters turn hazardous
waste into silos of fertilizer to spread
over pastures.

The land is awash with illness. The tools
that wound and heal, gone: the disk of sun
no longer sacred,

the feathered lance in an undusted museum,
unvisited, the well a dry hole; no trickster
god to turn away pestilence.

Nothing turns, nothing transforms.
No one comes to ask whom we serve,
why we bleed.

2013:

My people are mostly gone. The town
has dwindled but nevertheless boasts a new
Christian coffeehouse

and a restored marble soda fountain.
And yet another remnant of the past
is to be "restored":

seas once rolled here leaving
salt as well as salt-tolerant grass.
And so this part

of the prairie, ignored, never leashed, spread out
and bloomed. For years deemed "wasteland,"
the salt marsh was left

alone to grow its network of roots
and seeds—its invisible bio-mass—
underground, where

fire and drought were never dangers.
Now tourists, driving through this reserve
can look through binoculars

at the diorama without even
leaving their cars. But today, a Tuesday,
this twenty-two-

thousand-acre remnant of the past
is chained shut by a government standoff
led by the single-minded,

giving me leave to walk in alone.
Disappointing daughter, I do not
disappoint this land.

It simply accepts my brief return,
allows me to unfold my wings,
then lets me go.

Short, brown stems of sunflower stretch
all the way to that old cedar;
dry, silver shells of

milkweed have opened to the wind.
Endangered whooping cranes rest here
on their way to elsewhere.

This is a place for those who wander, whose
jeans will carry sand burrs to
another place: who,

like the wind, do not mean to stay.
I bless the cottonwood glinting gold,
the meadowlark riffling

his song, the gleaming bull snake
warming her long body in the sand
before slipping

into the tall grass. I mix
with all my relatives:
the many-minded—

mouse, deer, coyote, fox, rabbit,
plover, pelican and crane standing and waiting
for fish. I call upon

the four directions to exalt the huge
grasshoppers that terrified me as a child:
the crickets that calmed,

the locusts that buzz even above the wind;
the great blue herons like the one
tattooed on my shoulder;

I call upon the center and feel the sand
ever shifting under my feet; I look
up at the clean

sun and all my winged, boundless relatives
wheeling on the wind, redeemers all,
turning, readying the world

for change as I, too, turn, step
back over the chain across the road
and go.

2014–2017

Family Snapshot

You sit at the center:
the older sister,
the only one of us smiling,
the only one composed, gazing
direct into the eye of the camera
as if to affirm (though the rest of us
won't know this for another month):
your life stands complete.

The rest of us are caught
somewhere in the midst of our lives,
perched on the porch steps.

We are blurred or blinking or glancing off
at the horizon or down at the dogs.
We have so many more things
to do. We can hardly wait to
shift, to be released from this enforced
immobility.

Grouped in still life, no one looks at
anyone else. No one touches. Unposed,
we suffer the shot in the thick
of our own separate, suspended lives.

Though we didn't see it then,
it's clear as the sky before a quake:
you were to become the core of our epic,
your approaching death
(forever after) our epicenter.

2011

Decoration Day—Kansas, 1953

South winds parch the land. Tractors claw it into grooves.
Blunt glass combs separate with long, monotonous strokes
the line wires bucked by the wind. Buckled by the driving wind,
once taut fence wires lean toward this forty-acre square.

Come in from sky to sky of hot, grey road and brown, dry,
crumbling earth to forty acres of unnatural green:
grass which curls around and chokes the native grass
while death spreads cancer-like across the graves, is cut off
at the rusty buckled joint of wire, as if the land once said
'This and no more can you have.'

Not so. The amputation fails. It spreads into the farmhouse
kitchen where, nerves frayed by the wind, timetables
kept within the hospital are parsed, dissected, shared in tones
reserved for other calendar events:
drought and summer harvest, fertilizer, grain.

Here, over death they silent stand—
sunburned men, tie-loosened, lean on dusty Chevrolets
in narrow ruts, looking, staring, wind would tear their words away.

Hot wind burns, constricts the throat, but warm spring spicket
water's for the dead. I must not press or step on mounded graves,
but which way, east or west, rest the heads?
Brass dirt-encrusted cups hold soldiers' tattered, shrunken flags.
My hand brushes the harsh stone wool of lambs;
their sightless eyes stare back. They stare beyond
the women's kneeling forms, beyond the wind-tossed line grove.

All tears, all moisture to the dead, no cup, no sound,
no fluid for the quick.
All forced down, hunched from the never-dying wind.
The meadowlark outside will not come in.
Gifts for the dead,
libations to the land and wind.

ca.1969, rev. 2023

After Easter Service, 1956

Idling in our new Buick waiting to leave
the parking lot with all the other colossal

cars exhaling soft invisible exhaust
into the thickening shadows of spring, the birth

season of small creatures not yet blighted
except by their own natures, my father lights up,

my mother stares as always inward to
her draped casket of sadness, me thinking,

from the back seat, my eleven-year-old
ankles encased in hose and properly crossed,

how the day I die will be a day
just like today, how each day

will become inexorably today, will
slide into yet another day

like beads on (we had no
rosaries) the cheap steel chain

clasping my cold war ID tag
tucked under the thin dress, or

better yet, I muse, like walking
backwards in between drops of rain,

or though there are no computers
then, like plunging link through endless

link until the day I die.
And it will be, I remember thinking

with some horror, on a day
just as real as today, when

I sit, without a seat belt, alone
on the wide back bench, quiet

so as not to startle those two
silent anxious adults scanning their own

bound worlds, so as not to call
their attention, though caged, so as

to be left alone, young spring
creature camouflaged inside its own

life, blessed with the instinct
to be very still, waiting to hang

the sweaty dotted Swiss up to dry,
waiting to slip on shorts, waiting

as patiently as I can until it's safe
for my real life to begin.

2005–2023

113

The Apparent Immortality of Things

Sometimes I catch them at it
alone in the house

catch sound of their stillness
their capacity to wait

their pointing to something beyond
passage, something

beyond loss. There is beauty
in their silence,

the way they allow
the slipcover of light

to flicker, to play over
their surfaces but never

themselves alter, never
change. Of course,

they do. But I rarely
see it: the slow

settling of grime into
a surface, the bleaching,

thinning of fabric by sun.
But to me

they just remain, never
moving, whether I'm

there or not, the same
when I return

from a day or a week or a month
away in the sweaty,

swirling world of eating
and breathing and pain.

Here they still are,
neither precisely

dead nor living,
stretching out,

present participles,
constant as mothers,

light and air and time
mapping such

tiny inroads my eyes
are too big, too

young, too tender
to see.

2011

Tying the Knot

—for Steve

I struggle, spread on the bow, sweat
dripping to wet fingerless gloves,

to tie a bowline in the stiff
slimed hulking rope of the mooring.

Patiently you have told me: "out
of the hole, round the tree, into

the hole" but line resists loop, hole
laps backwards or rabbit

runs round the tree widdershins
and under my hands falls away

to nothing. Neither has my double
hitch held, the second twist

taking a wrong turn, sliding
free, unsnagged, deep

into churning water. You've tried
to show me how to plait the figure

eight, infinite knot holding
firm under stress but in calm,

slipping free. I've shrunk from the bright
beam of love's dazzling ring,

that lasso's unwavering light.
I've shied from enclosure, cheered when

the cowpoke's lariat falls
flat. Yet how tenderly

you would wrap a tasseled cord
round the skittish bones of my wrist

then your own as we'd lace
vows; you'd lead me, blindfolded

mare from a blazing barn,
lash me like that other sailor

to a mast of trust. Show me,
my Houdini, once again

how to tie that automatic
knot, how bitter ends

come naturally to connection,
how blunt, blind fingers find

the way to links that simply last
or loosen on command, even

in the dark of inattention,
even under water, even

in a sunken trunk bound with
leather straps, even as,

expert, lithe, adept, we brim
with, hold each other's breath.

Teach me that.

2004

Picking Peaches

My mother remembered one beautiful day.
She pilgrimed with others to pick bushels
of peaches in the public orchard, and after,
she would can jam and bake pies,

but that wasn't the point. The point was
the glory of that day, the rare harmony
with her husband and their friends, the warmth and
lusciousness of the just-picked fruit.

For once, she allowed herself happiness,
or rather, delight overtook her.
But next year when they returned, angels
of Eden barred the way with swords: the day

wasn't quite as warm, her husband in a
foul mood, the peaches sour, pithy,
overripe. She always talked about
her disappointment as if she just couldn't

understand why, once allowed,
a particular pleasure couldn't be recaptured,
but bounded away into the past.
Yet she rounded up sorrows easily,

pecks of sad skinny cats always
at the back door, a yowling litany
she thought would leave her alone, if she fed them.
Instead, they grew sleek and fat. I saw

they would never leave a good thing
once they found it. My mother-in-law never
used any beautiful thing she was given
but closed them all carefully away in drawers.

Released into dementia, she was never
disappointed by lining up present and past.
"What a beautiful garden," she would exclaim from
our porch, while she could still speak. And

a moment later, "What a beautiful garden,"
not knowing she was repeating herself.
The Buddhists say to meditate on death,
so to self-medicate against

forgetfulness of impermanence, a kind
of caffeine or nitroglycerin for the
soul. But like most mothers I have
no need to meditate on impermanence—

have seen moments snatched, fade, sucked
away right before my eyes, have
no belief that today's delights will last
past this turn of the kaleidoscope.

It seems joy is just something we pick.
I used to lick the warm fuzz of dust
off my mother's closed bedroom door.
My mouth still waters at the thought.

2008

119

Rose Sacrament

The white wooden trellis bowed
under their red weight in late May.
My mother rose when it was not yet
blistering hot to cut the clusters,

bind them, fill a dozen coffee cans
saved all winter, covered with tinfoil.
My father drove, Mother and I always
sitting in silence through drought-ravaged

Kansas to the cemeteries of Great Bend,
Hutchinson, Stafford, where
one or two cans, topped off with warm
water from the lone tap in brown buffalo grass,

were screwed into the hard, cracked clay
next to each gray stone chiseled with a family name.
I found the roses' scent sickening,
overripe in the stifling, fenced

enclosures of loss. I would not shed
tears for my sister for many years.
I never knew three of my grandparents.
As I fidgeted and played on stone lambs,

my mother stood silent before her best
offering, pricked fingers wrapped in Band-Aids.
As our car crunched away, I never looked back
but saw the roses already opening

their hidden parts, easy victims,
to the harsh wind. They would never
hold together long, readily offering up
their bared hips, their untethered ghosts.

True sacraments are hard to come by.
I should have paid better attention.

2012

Telling the Truth

I called my mother up yesterday
inviting her over to this side:
she forever 69, I edging toward 75.

She took a seat in the Adirondack chair
next to mine, looked me in the eye and listened
as I told her, for the first time, truth.

I said I could not lug any farther her stones
of guilt, the knots of loss she had left,
I thought, for me to carry on.

The stones were growing older, heavier.
The knots grew tighter. I had
no free hands to untangle them.

That was it. That was all I had to say.
She listened, nodded, the sun
glinting on her glasses. Finally

we turned from each other at precisely
the same moment, swung our heads like cows,
gazed across the prairie to the hills.

2019–2023

Giving Way

A friend continues to see signs of a departed husband:
a book drops out of the case, opens
to a poem both loved.

A cherished brother leaves heads-up dimes everywhere,
heralding his continuing presence and jaunty
affection from the afterlife.

This has never happened to me.
My dead are just gone, my problem, even if only
the goodbyes left up in the air.

There must be a name for this low-flying fear:
knowing we must give way to deaths
that will inevitably come, as well

as deaths a long time gone. Today,
a mourning dove whose call I've always feared
just as I feared my mother's constant sadness,

silently approaches, lands on my backyard deck rail
scattered with seed, slips her black-tipped wings
neatly into place.

As I sit here, outside, despite fall's rapid cooling,
she eats, glancing my way every few seconds,
then jitters toward the dark blue dish of water,

her bright black eyes ever checking
to see if either of us should be spooked
before she drinks her fill.

2021

On Your Birthday

—for Althea, 1908–2004

The graveyard's pocked with flowers that cannot die.
I want to sweep and lay my annuals here.
The cars rush past just short of where you lie.

Stones carved with sentimental lies
must make loss easier for some to bear,
like stocking the graveyard with flowers that cannot die.

My dahlias will last a little, for I pry
a rusty spigot open while I hear
the cars rush past just short of where you lie.

At the busy curb, then back inside,
I'll join the closed-up stream that shuts out fear
and litters graveyards with flowers that cannot die.

My bodies of blossoms will open to bees and flies
who light, exploring the rarely scented air
as cars rush past just short of where you lie.

I came to bring you what I cannot buy
even though I think you do not care
that graveyards fill with flowers that cannot die
and cars rush past just short of where you lie.

2005

Leavening

Listen: everything can be used.
Everything is a path;
even your grief

can curl into the center
where like a shard
of beached glass

worn that way and this
is wave softened at last.
Begin anywhere

and watch it start
to roll, to wash
into something

else, somewhere away
from the static ground
of winter doubt into the chaotic

order of a cloudy spring. Only part
of the picture, peace
spreads slowly.

The debris of self-pity,
consumed by winter-famished
Kali, is the leaven

by which we rise, the tiptoe lightning
of laughter on the edges of fronts,
the thresholds of thunder on which, teetering, we see.

Look: here is balm for your tangled
clump of self-sorrow, this flight of steps

stretching from the bare bottom
of this ridiculous snuffling pig

of our humanity to what is called
paradise. Hung on this laddered cross

between fleet summer grass and
ancient flare of stars,

we look down, up:
where build our home?

Come: rising
from cavern to heaven,

mounded earthen birds

between soil and sky,
we escape:

unpinioned, we grow wings.

Yeast bubbles in our bones
which lighten, fill

with air. Our throats

inflate with song. We flow
into feathered capes,

sacrifice sorrow; birds of flame,

we are restored in ash-filled nests;
we soar, doves of mourning.

Carving air with wings we learn

to slip qualms, recover stalls,
move from here to there

by naked intention.

Called down to bury her once more,
we forfeit flight but never lose

the leavened feel of space,

the sill of sight, the truth
of unthinkable migrations

height substantiates.

                                                    2011

She Holds Her Tongue

i. Stop

After years of pleading,
quarreling, wheedling,
haranguing, intervening,
the record has slowed
to a stop.

She is silent.

A stroke has scrambled her tongue.
Or a tracheotomy tube fills her mouth.
Or sorrow halts everything.

In the silence that follows the
failure of words she stares
at the ceiling.

Holding her tongue
in her mute mouth,

she watches the dumbshow
of her life distilled
in a can of film.

Only her eyes move.

She looks up: sees
what she has struggled
to mirror.
The reflecting pool clears.

Dismembering all she has learned,
she uncouples her bones
from the muscles of her mistakes:
begins again.

ii. Start

In the silence that follows
sacrifice, one by one

the buds of her fingers
bloom,
ripple,
strengthen in separateness,
grow dexterous and supple
in autonomy.

Her head pulls sideways,
attending to inaudible
translations.

Parts of her, like offspring,
cradled separately,
listen,
come alive,
learn to pronounce
their own truth.

Suddenly set free,
an ear soliloquizes;
a thigh sympathizes;

a knee drones;
a knuckle overhears;
the belly laughs;
a breast points to the moon.

Her body's life
becomes a grammar
she roots through.

Her hands paint
her face white,
lips red, pull
a knitted cap over
her howling skull.

Steadily, she recollects
herself; the tuning fork of
her body begins to resound.

The whisper of silent
voices she acknowledges
(but doesn't recognize)
as hers.

Like ice melting on a creek,
she loosens, is less invested,
can slip, murmuring, over rocks,
fluent in many tongues.

The poem of her body
becomes a round,
an antiphonal chorus,
whole in any part.

An always moving
melody, the center builds, releases
to limbs, returns
to the lips: utters
intricate truth.

2001–2011

Called Back

A little too tardy in coming back to my call, my shepherd wags
her slow, apologetic shuffle to my feet

to be scolded, sorry grin on her face,
head down, solicitous eyes on my face.

No real urgency curtailed her romp, just
the tyranny of my impatience, my need to be obeyed.

What makes me think I have this right, I ask,
making her revisit sit, stay, come, as if

she had forgotten how, not that she had merely
momentarily surrendered to some intriguing delight as I

even, sometimes, allow myself to do but only when I ignore
the clocks. Later, in a carpeted patch of sun,

we lie together, settling, while she licks
my thumbs and fingers, not begging pardon, not because

they taste of salt, but because they claim attention—palms and
bony backs—because through the puppy skin of vestigial webs,

they need, blind babies, to be nudged back to the capacious now,
from the wandering sadness of being human, a long way away.

2000–2023

She Folds Laundry

Sun-dried shriveled hands
flashing rings with sprung settings,
they have come to this:
humped over an old-woman smell,
folding other people's laundry.

Unhurriedly she smooths,
presses each piece,
flattens, turns,
multiplies dimension.

Long fingers prop fabric
into fanciful forms:
a long-beaked bird,
the dragon in the mirror,
the dog flopping asleep on her bed,
the hornet bumping against glass.

She looks back down
at the clean towel on her lap
considering its shape
while a spider in the corner
crochets its web.

In silent mimicry she thinks,
like you they crimp possibility
into the same old nets,
tuck thought into tight
packets of words: hook, weave
pleat from their programmed spinnerets.

She smiles, creasing
the soft mesh of diapers
warm, soft, and sweet,
seducing the cheek.

Flesh flowers and withers,
fills and wrinkles,
time doubling back materially
as sideways she sees her own
young mother through the door watch her
with that worried look.
The weave of her love would never stretch
as far as this old woman, she thinks:
these folds no longer dimpled, kissable,
but slack, hung from brittle bones.

She stacks intricately plaited textiles
back into the basket so that light
tips radiance across many layers.

It will not last,
she thinks.
The moment it is donned
it comes undone,
the inexact geometry
of tomorrow's universe
unfolding.

I ply cloth but
who has shrunk this
life called mine
into such pinched shape
even light can't love?

2008

Homeless in August

The new bed rests where the old
one was, but he will not
set paw on its new-smelling
softness—instead, sticks his nose under
the old rug wadded for trash, sighs
at what still smells like home.

Moved to the Alzheimer's unit, your mother,
bereft of smell and direction, pleads,
"I just want to go home."
And again, over and over again,
"Let me go home. Please.
Please, take me back home."

Home was my big sister,
how easy we were together,
laughing, wrestling, dabbing our sweaty wrists
and necks with "Evening in Paris."
One night she complained of headache,
took two days to die from polio.

This is a kinder August. The locusts
sing a less threatening song.

After years of commuting, you are home.
Red, fragrant flowers blossom from our walls.

With luck, their scent will stay
while comfort, like August, will come, will go.

2014–2023

133

For Mary

(1917–2003)

Time tightens about us both,
but for you, it's like a ring of light
shrinking to a tiny circle
of present, holding you here.

Tomorrow you will not remember
our talk about your spinster aunt
who laughed at men,
or how you chortled, telling it,

or how you listened to me play,
the only one present hearing
Mozart as if for the first time,
or how, after, like mad royalty,

you sat on the porch alone,
refusing to come in, feeling
the fierce rain, its strength
somehow bringing you peace.

Tomorrow will wipe all that away
and you will rise from your bed,
exclaiming at the lilies, asking me
what are they called.

Holding your hand, I struggle
to enter that circle with you,
to hear what speaks from that center
that does not move.

ca. 1995–2023

She Ponders Questions of Quantum Physics

i. Schrödinger's Cat

Stay with the hard questions,
I say severely to my
self in the mirror.

Like Schrödinger's cat
you have only a tendency
to exist. All depends

on what you're looking
for, what you believe
possible.

Old women are liminal,
I mutter; you can become
anything.

My mother once told me this;
she was lying then;
perhaps not now.

Daily, someone must see
the sun
up.

What Lady, what Tiger
stands behind the door
of your expectation?

What is the meaning
of choice?
Which future blooms

because of your thought?
Curiosity actually keeps
the cat alive;

a greying particle
of pussy grins,
disappears.

ii. Strange Attractors

Meaning remains the strange
attractor
of my life.

It dances like Gene Kelly
on the horizon, beckoning
me, closer now.

I am no choreographer:
a life's improvised steps
take on the pattern,

the coloring
of soul's vision.
Stumblings across stage

have a grace and balance
of design not soon apparent
to the critical house of youth.

Small choices, turns,
gestures encompass consequence
beyond conception.

Love is the pull
drawing us to momentary
postures

holding past and future
in textured
interlocking rings

until they fall away
like heavy jewels from Buddha's
long lobes.

iii. Uncertainty Principles

You cannot be measured.
Just when you think
you know who and how big

you are,
you take a quantum leap
to somewhere else

to appear larger
or smaller than you
were.

Never check your watch,
count your money,
gauge your progress.

Don't look under the bed,
assume the worst,
look back.

Burn measuring sticks of all
kinds with their proud
certainties.

Drop-outs and fairy tale
heroines have always
known this. Physicists

in solemn white coats assess,
shake heads, shrug, spread
their large hands.

iv. parallel   universes

what is the meaning
of a choice
do you want to see

                                                  a black hole
                                                  under the
                                                  skirt
                                                  of woman

                                                  Pluto fears
                                                  the vagina
                                                  that sucks
                                                  men

into eleusis
where time
rushes backwards effect

loops around cause
where a small flicker
creates a cleft universe

                                                  bifurcation
                                                  is built
                                                  into the
                                                  infinity
                                                  of our very
                                                  bodies

shadowing
us
wherever we
go
like
amoebas

we split the skin
of our egos
again and again

and do not die
seeds are useful
only when cracked

tulips bloom
only
after being
frozen
future's
echo

informs
her choice
to cleave

this spring
smoothly
along lines
she has
chosen

is it possible
yet not to know
these robins

pecking among the rubble
of winter for ruby pits
these turquoise tips barely seen

of what are amethyst iris
golden lilies did they also
sunder the spring she left

                                        her mother
                                        it seemed a smooth
                                        road
                                        inevitable the other
                                        slender
                                        possibility
                                        shriveling
                                        like an umbilical but

has she
also traveled
that road

to come to the end of youth
now growing old apart
mother daughter

like rhizomes our
possibilities grow too thick
and must divide

                                        for space to
                                        grow
                                        together and
                                        Proserpine
                                        ever green

has never left
we cleave so we
may cleave and

i lift my skirt
and grin
ceres raises

her stricken face
to smile silken
rolls of spring

                                        instantly
                                        unfurl
                                        from one

                                        perfect
                                        seamless
                                        speck

                                        2000–2023

Mixing Cement

—for Rachel

They are surprisingly heavy
as your Uncle Phil and I hoist the 60-pound bags,
lug them to the trough
one at a time, rip them open,
darken the grey powder
with water, then blend
with the hoe till the mixture of
limestone, sand, and gypsum glops.

Then we tip and trowel sixteen of these,
sweat dripping from our foreheads,
into four round cardboard tubes,
each four feet deep, the wet cement plopping
and echoing deep as an outhouse, then
mounding at the top like mud pies
into which we center one inverted bolt.

From the kitchen, from the quick clean distant expectations
of youth, you scrutinize us narrowly as we work
slowly but methodically, so the goop won't start
to set before it's poured, and I remember
at fifteen feeling my life so malleable,
nothing had fused, I could be
anything, though impatient
at gradually being cast into
roles whose functions
I could not fathom.

Yet, like you,
I had already sexed and named my unborn children,
chosen and dressed my paper doll bridesmaids.
As an afterthought, you've picked the name of your groom,
know where you will study the one particular subject,

the single specific way the world will be better
because you have lived.

I rest against the hoe, despite legs flecked with stinging cement,
soles choked with mud, nails ragged and clotted with clay, hair
       askew, and look back
at the sturdy unforeseen shapes my life has taken and at the neat,
elegant, ghostly blueprints of dwellings unbuilt, and know

that the atoms of callow convictions are a concrete fast to set,
that only time's revolving reactor can smash them, its fission
freeing fabulous quirks and quarks, belongings yet undreamed.

Washing the harsh alkali from my flesh, I muse that maybe even
yesterday's fluid forms continue to be conceived and poured, and
       wish for you, cast into earth's extended exile,
an un-envisioned future, its fallen frames more fortunate,
more fitting, than any pure, still fixture of Eve's perfect garden.

2003–2023

Keeping Company with the Figment of Blue

—for Jessi

As the blue jay flew
  ahead of us through the woods,
    you said, from the new
      purlieu of adulthood,

you know,
its blue is a figment: a mere construct
of feathers and light.

I did know, wanted to say
  I did know but did
    not say it, having mostly learned
      when not to speak;

having loved
  that bird and its blueness;
    having made it yours
      since that distant day I held you
        up to the sky in woods like these and heard
          its blue *skreee* mix with your cry.

Figments spread color between
the broad black outlines of every day,
big fat pigments teasing delight
from the sun's prism that we hoard and parse:
my favorite always the mystery
of blue, deepening into purple and out,
or circling back
into the powerful ram of red.

All that I know I don't know
keeps me company, sits with me
in moments of ease like an old friend.

Today this jay
lands and takes off
          from branch to branch
then darts into what we can never know.

I watch you watch it dip black-barred wings,
then pivot, its flash of blue
falling slant to the sun.

ca. 2007

Single Truths

—for Liana

In depths of arrogance invisible pirates nod, unseen, except
when their defenses slip, certain they know the single
truth of doom. At thirteen, under their spell, a Wendy
waking to all the current Hooks of horrors, fixed
victim slipping down Peter's sodden plank of Panic
with no wings, rope, sword, no buoyant shield, how dare I
tell you that all can be well, that we do learn but only
from failure, that hearts can recover, polluted oceans clear,
slashed trees re-sprout once we see, without the dark
one-eyed patch of fear, what we unthinkingly have done?

You never saw fire fly till last night from our blacked-out porch
when you glimpsed a single spark of flashing light. What's that?
you gasped, pointing. Long past the hot dusks of my childhood
when we ran to catch these living jewels to twist them
into cruel bright rings, I tell you that we poisoned them with spray.
The Japanese believe these sparks to be souls of the dead
called to rekindle light become extinct in drained fields and woods.

In my need for you to be happy, I want to say,
close your eyes; recognize that once-unbelievable fact:

you can fly if you move forward faster than you fall.

ca. 2000

Skullcap

—for Jessi, Rachel, and Liana

We lie swaddled inside the late August tent,
you dropping easily into the arms of night.
Earlier we curled, cocooned,
watched through mesh, listened to the bluster of heaven.

Now the rain has gone. Wind blows full
across the moon. Softly I unzip the door,
step out into what I have sought
to protect myself from: this wild

clarity of moon, this profusion of stars.
The night is another country.
I need to cover my skull with a cap to keep
something between me and eternity.

When you were a babe, soft spot still
knitting, you startled when undressed, flailed
your limbs until bundled, gathered in together.
                    On the verge of puberty,

I glimpsed a universe through great lenses
on Mt. Palomar and couldn't sleep for weeks
until I believed again in gravity, the kind
I now know doesn't exist.

We are not gathered into earth's arms after all;
we are liquid ribbons poured from the dark
pitcher of space and time.
                    On the night I was first married,

we slept open to the sky in a field in Canada.
All night, a passenger traveling east,
I watched great patterns of stars wheel their way west.
                    This is the month of decay

when pods start to unravel, blow apart,
but for now, you and I float
on a brimming font. Even so
you're drifting away, deeper into

your own time, waxing into the space
of next month's moon. I'm thinning,
flying into a moonless night, last
chakra flung open, pieces of bone

never quite fit, like continents set adrift.
Somewhere in these depths a new eye buds,
its lid thins, becomes translucent. In time,

perhaps it will dilate, see in the dark.

ca. 1990–2023

148

Charades

—for Alden and Alex

The first day following them around
while their parents are in Paris
expecting me to feel in charge
leaves me feeling

six and a half decades slip off as
easily as a hot, heavy, pointless coat and there
I am again,
nine,

the three of us bucking on creaky
chain swings, me pumping legs
wildly shouting come on!
come on!

and on the makeshift stage
taking my turn at animal
charades, moving as I've seen
it move:

loping on long legs in the empty
morning park, cousin distant to my
domestic dog, its shaggy unleashed neck
held high,

sniffing the air, daring us, not caring
that it's seen, not afraid of anything, and both boys—
lean, pre-adolescent bodies taut and ready—
greedily pounce:

"Coyote! My turn!"

2018

Forty Years of Love—An Abstract

—for Steve

They end by filling in one another,
something recalled from the very last time,
each with its own before and after, a new
wash of color layering their likeness of love

something recalled from the very last time,
one begins by touching the other's mouth,
a wash of color layering their likeness of love
how the pale or dark fullness invites

her to begin by touching his lower lip
before the first time she watched its shape,
how the pale or dark fullness invited
the wet trace of her index finger, her tongue

before the last time she watched the lip
of him become more defined, like a rubbing
after she traced it with her finger or tongue, as
a rubbing on stone, on pale granite

becomes more defined, like a tracing
he touches her breast as if for the first time,
like a rubbing on stone, on pale granite
the papery flesh receiving the wash of his tongue,

he touches her breast as if for the last time,
its gravity, its curve, drawing him into its pale
papery flesh receiving the wash of his tongue
the dark aureole the color of emptiness

its gravity, its curve, drawing him into its pale
memory of thin blue milk washing over him
dark aureole the color of emptiness,
faint moon of its outline fills and depletes,

memory of thin blue milk washing over him
still, though their children are full grown
faint moons of their outlines fill and deplete
as they enter the other once again,

though their children are not yet born, still
they join in a different wash, a different blend
as they enter the other once again
a new combination, new creation

they join in a different wash, a different blend
before the womb is gone, after it's gone
a new combination, new creation
always a just completed thing, replete,

before the womb is gone, after it's gone,
before the bright white wash of time,
never a just completed thing, replete
after the overlay: a thickening of surprise

before the sharp quick lime of time
with its shallow before and after, a new
overlay, another thickening of surprise:
they start by filling out one another.

2005–2023

A Question of Time

i.

Nine thousand years seems long but for the imagination: see
a Siberian girl smile as she reaches out to touch the sagittal crest
(*shaped like an arrow, indicating strong jaw muscles*) on the head
of a Husky, once-removed from wolf, panting by the fire
after pulling home a sled of reindeer meat.

Now, see them both die (you can fill in the cause),
buried in a single grave, discovered just last year.

Time (*Anglo Saxon: timma, tide*) streams through us,
modifying species and individuals little by little.
At birth our innocent lungs fill with air, with time:
sails catching a breeze, seedlings thrusting up watery green stems,
rushing through the detritus of April, pushing up, thickening until
the instant the fatal blossom explodes at the tip.

Time is older than the oldest language, its silence older
than its creatures' utterances, attempted expressions of their lives;
it travels through some bodies faster than others, leaving behind
sloughed shapes, unfinished shadows; it has moved through each
of my Three Dogs seven times faster than through me.

ii.

Two hundred years of selective breeding have spawned
a monstrous array of creatures called 'dogs,' becoming
ever fitter for human purposes, including friendliness and
laboratory testing. Eighty-four percent of our DNA is the same.

Sixteen percent remains unknown, useless to the other, wild.
Guns are quick to put down useless animals.

This morning I see a man whip a large Scottish Terrier
(*bred to rid farms of vermin and to help seize game*)
with the leash he carries; the giant dog refuses to heel.
I stare hard at the man's back, my limbic brain shooting
fight, then flight, then powerlessness, then, from my newer
frontal lobe, hope he will eventually change.

He calls to mind my father, fifty years ago, whipping
his Brittany Spaniel (*bred in France as gun dogs*).
When often in memory I scream at him to stop, he always
drops the rolled-up newspaper, ever surprised.

iii.

My Last Dog is a mix of Husky (*sled pullers, guards, hunters)*
and German Shepherd (*search-and-rescue, police, and military).*

Thirteen years seems long except for the imagination.
My children grown, I find myself before the cages
at the shelter just to look. They say I am too old
for the adolescent handsome male I have chosen,
categorized on his cage as "orange," meaning
he needs lots of exercise.

Incensed at their assessment of me, I pay to take Last Dog home.
And though they are correct in that I cannot run as fast as he,
they do not know that he will come to lope beside my bike,
the two of us, pulled by instinct and imagination, a team
in the Iditarod.

At 62, I believe Last Dog and I might live out our lives
        alongside one another.
At 75, it does not seem so likely.

iv.

Time is stealthy (*Anglo Saxon: stehlen, to steal*).
Eight thousand years seems long but for the imagination.
Hear Lao Tzu speak: *time makes possible all that is;*
what allows us to live, permits us to die.
Walt Whitman insists, a mere 150 years gone,
death is different from what anyone supposes, and luckier.

I am counting on luck: composing a detailed script for when
time is nearly through with me but pain is not. If I can catch
that sweet spot I will not eat or drink. This is called suicide,
though if someone withholds nourishment at my behest,
it is termed murder (*to rub away; harm*);
both are sins (*synne, of unknown origin*).

Dogs may be bred for aggression, but they never
hold their breath, imagining death. They do not anticipate.
We do.

In liver sausage he never refuses, I hide antibiotics for the sepsis
that leaves Last Dog trembling, feverish,
after each chemo treatment.

The palliative prednisone makes him manic, knocking coasters
off the coffee table with his nose, in a replay of his puppyhood
I never saw. I am patient. I cook meals twice a day and he eats,
voraciously, pisses constantly.

He is anxious, panting for something I'm not ready to give.
Never bred for displays of affection, now he pushes
his head into my lap relentlessly, asking, asking.

v.

It is just a question of time.
Restoring Last Dog, me, or, in fact, the earth that together
we've explored, to health is out of the question.

I compose another script.

I will hire his murderer: rely on a stranger
with her needle of oblivion to force time to unleash
Last Dog's body as painlessly as possible, leaving me
(for we will of course have separate graves), for a time,
still alive, attended by his completed shadow.

This leaves the heavy grief *(grever: to weigh down, afflict)*
all of us must carry, in proportion to our given
length of life,
breadth of vision,
depth of (what else to call it?)
love.

2020

Red Cedar

It first appeared out front by the curb
two inches high, some kind of evergreen.
I thought to let it grow, but knew
it would most likely be mown down.

I put it in a pot and moved it to the lawn.

It grew. It grew so fast it couldn't stay there long.

Finally, I brought it here, to the back yard,
already crowded with my ill-chosen giant
lilacs, (invasive) honeysuckle,
spirea and forsythia (no light),
rampant daylilies that never bloom, wandering
raspberry canes and wild rhubarb
I've tried to keep in check.

I dug a hole in the back corner by an unused gate,
after I looked up to make sure there was room to grow.
I set at-hand bits of brick and stone around its trunk
to hold it steady, pulled the wild canes away in summer,
the snow off its flattened branches in winter.

I went back to talk to it today, this June afternoon,
to tell it how lovely and fast it has grown—
now just my height.

One day someone else may love it, or, at the very least,
let it be.

2023

About the Author

Kathleen A Dale's prize-winning poems have appeared in many journals and anthologies. She is the author of three chapbooks, two full-length books of poetry, and an autobiography. She has been interviewed by various literary journals and has won several best-of-issue awards.

In 2022, Dale's poem, "The Final Thing" (now titled "First Dive"), placed first in the Kelsay Books' Women's Poetry Contest in partnership with the International Women's Writing Guild. In 2021, her poem, "A Question of Time," was one of only six nominated by *Rattle* for the Pushcart prize—her second nomination.

Dale is a native of Kansas, where she published her first poem and began the lifelong practice of keeping a journal. She received a BA in English at Ohio Wesleyan University and an MA in English Language and Literature at the University of Michigan. Settling in Milwaukee, Wisconsin, she earned the PhD in Modern American Poetry at the University of Wisconsin-Milwaukee where she then taught writing courses for non-regularly-admitted students for 26 years.

Since retiring, she has taught poetry workshops to at-risk teens, military veterans, and others. For the past six years, Dale has professionally mentored adult poets of all ages, both in the United States and abroad, from whom she receives much inspiration!

You can find more about her work, hear her read,
and email her through her website at:
kathleenanndale.com

Dale is also an amateur pianist who began lessons at age seven and continued through high school at Wichita State University. In late middle age, she returned to her studies at the Wisconsin Conservatory of Music. There, she has performed five recitals featuring the compositions of contemporary women.

You can hear excerpts at:
soundcloud.com/kathleenann45

Dale and her husband, Steven Kapelke, have three grown daughters and two grandsons.

Made in the USA
Monee, IL
03 April 2024

56126707R00089